THE MONSTERS
AND CREATURES OF GREEK MYTHOLOGY

by Don Nardo

COMPASS POINT BOOKS
a capstone imprint

Compass Point Books
151 Good Counsel Drive
P.O. Box 669
Mankato, MN 56002-0669

Editors: Sarah Eason and Geoff Barker
Designers: Paul Myerscough and Simon Borrough
Media Researcher: Susannah Jayes
Content Consultant: Michael Vickers, DLitt., Professor of Archaeology, University of Oxford
Production Specialist: Laura Manthe

Image Credits
Alamy: The Art Gallery Collection 42–43, 48, Erin Babnik 16, bilwissedition Ltd & Co. KG 15,
Christopher Griffin 5, Images & Stories 8–9, Ivy Close Images 18, Mary Evans Picture Library 36–37,
Nigel Reed QED Images 24–25, Liam White 6; **Bridgeman:** National Museum, Damascus, Syria/ Peter
Willi 53; **Corbis:** Arte & Immagini srl 10; **Geoff Ward:** cover (front), 12–13, 23, 31, 40–41, 50, 54–55;
Photolibrary: IBL Bildrya 32–33; **Shutterstock:** Allesandro0770 chapter 2 bgd, 60, Almotional 1,
Amici 58 (goat), Aquatic Creature chapter 3 bgd, 58–59 bgd, 64, Nadezhda Bolotina chapter 1 bgd,
62 bl, Brandon Bourdages 25 r, Cattallina 58–59 (woman), Cenker Atila 58–59 (man), Stephen Chung
56–57, Svalbona Gintaras 58–59 (lion), Eugene Ivanov 38 (front), Janprchal 46, Panos Karapanagiotis
4 r, 62 r, Nickolay Khoroshkov 3, chapter 4 bgd, KUCO 34, Daniela Migliorisi 26–27, Sean Nel cover
(back), Oksanika 58–59 (horse), Michael Onisiforou 28–29, Pio3 59 (bull), Davor Pukljak 45, Fesus
Robert 38–39, Sdecoret 58–59 (eagle), James Thew 20–21, Ylq 58–59 (snake).

Library of Congress Cataloging-in-Publication Data
Nardo, Don, 1947–
  The monsters and creatures of Greek mythology / by Don Nardo.
     p. cm. —(Ancient Greek mythology)
  Includes bibliographical references and index.
  ISBN 978-0-7565-4481-2 (library binding)
1. Monsters—Juvenile literature. 2. Greek mythology—Juvenile literature. I. Title. II. Series.
  BL795.M65N37 2012
  398.210938—dc22   2011015246

Visit Compass Point Books on the Internet at *www.capstonepub.com*

Printed in the United States of America in Stevens Point, Wisconsin.
082011
006341R

TABLE OF CONTENTS

Chapter 1

WHERE REALITY AND FANTASY DISSOLVE

Nearly every ancient human culture developed its own personalized mythology. Each mythology was a group of stories about gods, monsters, and human heroes. The heroes interacted with the gods and fought and killed the monsters. The typical mythology also contained tales about giants and incredible creatures with multiple heads or arms.

The peoples who created these fantastic stories knew little or nothing about science. They were highly superstitious. Also, they were mostly ignorant of the structure of the universe and how nature works. So they manufactured their collections of myths as a way of explaining the wonders of the universe and nature. Such stories told where fire, lightning, and thunder came from, for instance. Myths also explained how animals and human beings were created. Usually these and other living things were said to have been fashioned by gods or other supernatural beings or forces. Myths also described what happened after people died. These stories commonly included depictions of the Underworld or other realms of the dead.

Strange and Dangerous Creatures

Like other ancient mythologies, that of the Greeks had its creation stories and tales about the Underworld. It also featured all sorts of strange, colorful, and dangerous creatures. Some were half-human and half-animal, such as the satyrs, which were half-goat. Such hybrids were usually not a threat to people, though they could be mischievous or pesky.

The early Greeks also told tales of wondrous, awesome creatures. Among them were horses and lions with wings, a goat whose horns were filled with fruit, and a gigantic serpent that a goddess ordered to guard an important temple. Such beings rarely posed a hazard to humans. Some of them even helped people to overcome evil or various obstacles. The famous flying horse, Pegasus, for instance, carried the valiant hero Bellerophon when he slew a hideous monster called the Chimaera.

Monsters Meet Their Match

The Chimaera was far from alone. In addition to some mostly harmless creatures, Greek mythology was full of repulsive, terrifying monsters. Some had several heads, while others had snakes for hair. Still others were giants who towered over humans. Nearly all of the monsters had a taste for human flesh or blood. In most cases these monsters died at the hands of fearless human heroes.

The powerful Griffin was a hybrid of the lion, considered to be the king of the beasts, and the eagle, the king of the birds.

Nearly every Greek myth featuring a dreadful monster also contains a muscular, agile hero. As a renowned expert on Greek mythology, Edith Hamilton, put it:

> The mythical monster is present in any number of shapes, but [such creatures] are there only to give the hero his reward of glory. What could a hero do in a world without them? They are always overcome by him.

Endlessly Entertaining

The monsters and strange and wondrous creatures populating the Greek myths did more than explain the workings of nature and supply opponents for heroic humans. These fabulous beings also provided the classical Greeks with almost endless entertainment. The term "classical Greeks" describes the inhabitants of Greece in the centuries just before and after 450 BC. Most of them believed that the monsters and other creatures of their myths had existed in the dim past. They often called that earlier, action-filled era the

The playwright Euripides wrote many great plays, including *Cyclops*.

Age of Heroes. Today historians call it Greece's late Bronze Age, lasting from about 1500 BC to 1150 BC.

The importance of ancient myths in diverting and amusing the ancient Greeks cannot be overstated. They told and retold the tales about Pegasus, the Chimaera, and other mythical creatures. Children heard these tales and acted them out for fun. Storytellers called bards recited the myths before crowds on street corners. Many of the same stories were transformed into theatrical plays by talented writers such as the Athenians Sophocles and Euripides.

The fun factor of the Greek myths survived the end of classical Greece and of ancient times as well. Greek mythology became popular again in late medieval times. Then early modern storytellers, including English playwright William Shakespeare, passed the myths along to later generations. Even today, in an age in which science and knowledge have mostly replaced ignorance and superstition, the creatures of Greek mythology remain quaint and compelling. The half-human hybrids, wondrous winged creatures, giants, and snake-haired monsters are still widely popular. In fact, they regularly entertain far more people today than they did in ancient times. A modern historian points out:

> One of the fundamental reasons for the creation and perpetuation of [these] myths [is that] we read them with pleasure. [They] have given us some of our most beloved sagas. Above all, [we remember them for leading] us into that realm of which [the Greeks] will forever be the masters, where reality and fantasy dissolve, and come together again as [the] immortal poetry [of myths].

Chapter 2

HALF-HUMANS AND OTHER ODD CREATURES

According to the ancient Greek storytellers, in the Age of Heroes there existed a race of beings called centaurs. Each had the upper body of a human, including a man's head, chest, and arms. But a centaur's lower body was equine. It featured four legs, ending in hooves, and a bushy tail.

Apollo's Offspring

A story from that era said that these odd-looking creatures had been spawned by a human named Centaurus. His father was the god Apollo. One of the most versatile of the Greek deities, Apollo oversaw prophecy, healing, poetry, archery, and music. The story claimed that Apollo once had an affair with an attractive nymph named Stilbe. She lived near Mount Pelion, in Thessaly. That region, in central Greece, was known for its many fine horses. Soon after her union with the handsome Apollo, Stilbe gave birth to Centaurus.

An alternative myth said that Centaurus was the son of a man named Ixion and a cloud that a god had disguised to look like a woman. Whoever Centaurus' parents were, as a young man he mated with several Thessalian mares. They then gave birth to the centaurs.

As it turned out, these horse-men did not reflect very well on their father or grandparents. A majority of the centaurs were vulgar, messy, and foul-mouthed. They spent much of their time partying, drinking, and telling one another jokes and racy stories.

Though crude, the centaurs were normally no threat to their human neighbors. In fact, the two races often got along quite well. One exception was when the horse-men got drunk, at which time they could get both unruly and quarrelsome.

Centaurs and Drink

A tribe of Greeks known as the Lapiths saw the drunken centaurs in action. The Lapiths dwelled in a part of Thessaly not far from the caves and groves where the centaurs made their own homes. The king of the Lapiths, Pirithous, was a warm, hospitable man. So when he was planning his wedding feast, he thought it would be a neighborly gesture to invite the centaurs.

Centaurs were well known for their short tempers and rowdy behavior, especially when drunk.

9

Most of the horse-men gladly accepted the invitation. At first the festivities were pleasant and cordial. But after a while the centaurs did what they did best. They partied hard and got drunk. Suddenly they started saying that they owned the Lapiths' land. Not only that, the centaurs owned the people who lived on that land. Although these claims were false, at that moment the tipsy horse-men believed them. So they tried to grab and run off with the Lapith women. One centaur, Eurytion, went so far as to seize Pirithous' bride, Hippodamia.

The Centauromachy

Some of the Lapith men tried to reason with the centaurs. But this proved fruitless. So the men lost their tempers, drew their swords, and attacked the centaurs. What had started as a happy celebration quickly turned into a bloody fight. The Lapith women were rescued but dozens of centaurs were killed or wounded in the process. Later Greeks called this battle the Centauromachy, which they frequently depicted in paintings and sculptures. Some of the magnificent sculpted figures on Greece's most famous temple—the Parthenon, in Athens—were Lapiths clashing with centaurs.

A Poor Host

Another peaceful occasion that escalated into a brawl between humans and centaurs involved the renowned Greek hero Heracles (Hercules to the Romans). One day the barrel-chested strongman was passing through an area in which many centaurs lived. A horse-man named Pholus recognized Heracles. Hoping to make a good impression, Pholus invited the traveler to dinner. Also invited were several other centaurs, who viewed Heracles as a celebrity and wanted to meet him.

Unfortunately for all involved, Pholus was not a very good host. Like most centaurs, he had poor table manners, and he didn't know how to treat human guests. As a result, Heracles felt offended. An argument erupted and it soon led to a fight in which some of the horse-men were killed. Pholus was among the casualties.

The Civilized Centaur

One of the centaurs was very much unlike his equine brethren. His name was Chiron and he lived in a large cave on a slope of Mount Pelion. A highly accomplished individual, he was known all across Greece for his kindness, compassion, wisdom, and generosity. Chiron was the son of Cronus, leader of the first race of gods, the Titans, and a nymph named Philyra. Among the civilized centaur's close friends was the god Apollo. Like Apollo, Chiron became adept at archery and the arts of healing and music.

Name:
Heracles

Roman name:
Hercules

Family:
son of Zeus and Alcmena

Known for:
great strength, courage, and honor in completing the 12 Labors of Heracles

Symbols:
heavy club, lion skin

Chiron's passions were very different from those of the other centaurs. He enjoyed teaching and the arts.

Because Chiron was so civilized and wise, kings, queens, and on occasion even gods, sent their sons to live with him in his cave. There he tutored them in all manner of physical and intellectual pursuits. As a result boys who already possessed much potential were able to realize it. They became outstanding or famous, or both, for their abilities and achievements. They included Achilles, the most formidable of the Greeks who fought at Troy; the great hunter Actaeon; Asclepius, the god of healing; and the hero Jason, who captured the fabulous Golden Fleece.

Release from Pain

As the son of a Titan, Chiron enjoyed the gift of immortality. However, he could feel pain. This became a serious problem when, according to legend, he tried to remove an arrow from a wounded fellow centaur. It turned out that the arrow had been dipped in poison. So when the tip scratched Chiron's finger, he became ill. His pain grew so terrible that he wanted to die, so he gave his immortality to someone else. Ancient accounts vary on who the recipient was. In this way the most famous and best-liked centaur died.

Griffins: Strange Beaked Beasts

Centaurs, satyrs, and flying horses featured prominently in ancient Greek art. Their images were frequently shown on vases, bowls, and walls. Another fabulous creature that appeared often in both paintings and sculptures was the griffin. It had the body of a lion and the head, wings, and beak of an eagle.

Griffins had no major roles in any Greek myths. But they were mentioned in several classical Greek writings. Supposedly they lived far to the north of Greece in a land few humans had visited. They were said to guard a large collection of gold and other valuables there.

It appears that Greek images of griffins were based on weird-looking skeletons found in the distant region, which was east of the Black Sea. The skeletons belonged to lion-sized animals with four legs. They also had big, birdlike beaks. Modern experts think these skeletons were those of a small dinosaur called the protoceratops. The Greeks knew nothing about dinosaurs, of course. So they did not realize the bones were millions of years old. They assumed they belonged to a bizarre creature still living beyond the Black Sea, and they called it the griffin.

The Satyrs

The members of another group of mythical half-human creatures were as fond of parties and merriment as most centaurs were. They were the satyrs, who were half goat. They had hooves, pointed ears, and small horns atop their heads. Ancient writers gave several conflicting versions of the satyrs' origins. Probably the most often cited one was that they were among the many grandchildren of King Phoroneus. The legendary founder of the city of Argos, he was said to have mated with a nymph. Their offspring produced many other nymphs and their brothers, the satyrs.

The satyrs' main role was to assist Dionysus, god of wine and the fertility of the soil. The ancient Greek historian Diodorus Siculus wrote:

> It is reported [that the satyrs] were carried about by him [Dionysus] in his company and afforded the god great delight and pleasure in connection with their dancing and their goat-songs. And, in general . . . the satyrs, by the use of devices [jokes, games, and so forth] which contribute to mirth, made the life of Dionysus happy and agreeable.

Party Animals

Because they spent too much time with Dionysus, the satyrs came to share some of his traits. One was a strong fondness for partying and drinking wine to excess. Others included playing pranks on gods and humans and chasing nymphs and women.

Name:
Dionysus

Roman name:
Bacchus

Group of gods:
Olympian

Family:
son of Zeus and Semele

Responsibility:
vines and fertility of the soil

Symbols:
wine cup, ivy crown

Half man and half goat, satyrs are usually described as seeking the pleasures of wine and women.

Famed Satyr

The most famous satyr was Silenus. He was to the satyrs what Chiron was to the centaurs. Like Chiron, Silenus was highly civilized, educated, and wise. Silenus was also known for his ability to foretell events. One myth said that he was the son of Pan, the god of shepherds and flocks. Another legend held that Silenus' father was the messenger god, Hermes. Still another ancient story claimed that the famous satyr tutored Dionysus when he was young. That supposedly explained why the god chose satyrs to be his chief attendants.

The wise and sophisticated Silenus became a father figure to his pupil Dionysus.

Name:
Midas

Roman name:
Midas

Family:
adopted by King Gordius
and goddess Cybele

Known for:
his so-called Midas
touch; his obsession
with gold led to his
being granted his wish
of turning anything he
touched into gold

Silenus and Midas

One of the most famous myths about Silenus involved King Midas, ruler of Phrygia, in Asia Minor (what is now Turkey). Midas was most famous for his greed for gold. In one story he gained the power to turn anything he touched into gold. But that included his food, which meant he could no longer eat. Having managed to rid himself of the "Midas touch," the Phrygian king decided that he wanted to learn the secret of human life. If he knew that secret, he reasoned, he could become all powerful. That would allow him to acquire limitless treasures.

Midas had heard that the satyr Silenus was extremely wise and possessed the gift of prophecy. So the king captured Silenus and drugged him. Then Midas demanded that his prisoner tell him all about the secret of human life.

Silenus smiled. First, the drugs had little effect on him. Second, he realized that the secret Midas sought was only hearsay and did not actually exist. So he decided to trick the greedy king. He told Midas that the secret of human life was not to be born in the first place. Moreover, if one had already been born, he or she should die as soon as possible. Midas walked away in a state of confusion. Desperately he tried to figure out how he could profit from what Silenus had told him. Meanwhile the crafty satyr returned home, happy in the knowledge that wisdom was always superior to greed and other human vices.

Pegasus: The Flying Horse

In addition to such half-human hybrids as centaurs and satyrs, the landscape of Greek mythology was strewn with awe-inspiring creatures. Some of them could soar through the air like birds. Of these, perhaps the most amazing, as well as the most beautiful, was Pegasus. It was able to fly because it had two enormous and powerful wings jutting out from just behind its shoulders. According to legend, Pegasus was born from the body or blood of the hideous monster Medusa. The hero Perseus had sliced off her

The winged horse Pegasus carried Bellerophon to kill the Chimaera.

head, which had snakes for hair. It might seem odd that such an ugly being as Medusa could spawn a creature as good-looking as Pegasus. The reason was that at the time of her death Medusa was pregnant with the offspring of the sea god Poseidon, who was quite handsome. That offspring was Pegasus.

Fighting the Chimaera

The most famous myth about Pegasus told of how it helped the valiant young hero Bellerophon slay a monster. A king had asked the youth to kill the Chimaera, a dreadful beast that had been terrorizing many villagers and farmers. Bellerophon reasoned that fighting the creature would be easier if he could attack it from above. For that he needed to ride an animal that could fly, and Pegasus seemed the best choice. So the young man set out to tame the flying horse. Fortunately for Bellerophon, the goddess of war and wisdom, Athena, gave him a magic bridle. He found Pegasus drinking from a spring in Corinth in south-central Greece and managed to place the bridle over the horse's head. That made it easier for Bellerophon to tame Pegasus.

Once the man and horse came to trust each other, they flew off to fight the Chimaera. Finding the repulsive creature, they suddenly swooped downward, taking it by surprise. It tried to defend itself but Pegasus swiftly sped over and around it, allowing Bellerophon to hack away at it with his sword. Finally the Chimaera crashed to the ground, gave a last bellow of defiance, and died.

After a series of other adventures, Pegasus ended up in the stables of Zeus, leader of the Greek gods. Legends claimed that Zeus later placed the magnificent creature in the sky as a constellation. There in the night sky people have admired Pegasus ever since.

Name:
Pegasus

Roman name:
Pegasus

Appearance:
horse with wings

Family:
son of the sea god Poseidon and the monster Medusa

Famous myth:
flying with Bellerophon to kill the Chimaera

Also famous for:
being transformed by Zeus into a constellation

Chapter 3

MULTITUDES OF MONSTROUS GIANTS

Many of the Greek myths featured giants. These enormous creatures came in many shapes and sizes, but all were larger than humans. Exactly why the Greeks had so many legends about giants is not known. But most modern experts believe that Greek thinkers and writers were fascinated by humanity's place in nature. Natural forces such as storms, earthquakes, and floods were much bigger than people and their towns. They could and often did overwhelm and destroy humans and their works. Giants were also large and destructive. They may have symbolized those huge natural forces. As scholar Michael Stapleton puts it:

> The myth of the struggle between the gods and the giants [and between humans and the giants] probably reflected a struggle either between barbarism and order, or between man and the violent forces of nature. It was a favorite theme with [ancient Greek] artists and poets.

The ancient Greeks believed that natural disasters and destructive weather were sometimes the work of giants.

The 100-handers

According to the Greek myths, giants existed long before the human race arose. Perhaps the earliest giants were the Hecantoncheries, or "100-handers." They earned this name because each had 100 arms. Each also possessed 50 heads, which must have been a bizarre and frightening sight.

There were three 100-handers—Cottus, Briareos, and Gyes. They were the sons of Gaea and Uranus, divine forces embodied in nature's structure. Gaea was the mighty spirit dwelling within Earth, including the land, mountains, and seas. She gave birth to Uranus. He then inhabited the fabric of the sky and controlled all the heavenly bodies within it. Gaea and Uranus mated and produced many children. Among them were the members of the first race of gods, the Titans, and the three 100-handers.

Cottus, Briareos, and Gyes were so big and strong that just about all living beings feared them. Even the giants' own father, Uranus, was afraid of them. In fact, soon after their birth he tried to shove them back into Gaea's womb. But this outlandish move failed. So Uranus later locked up the 100-handers in Tartarus, the deepest, darkest part of the Underworld. Their mother eventually freed them. But the leading Titan, Cronus, so feared what they might do to him and his kind that he tossed them back into Tartarus.

The monstrous 100-handers scared their father Uranus so much that he imprisoned them in the Underworld.

Guarding the Titans

In time Cronus' son, Zeus, decided to overthrow the Titans. It was widely known that the 100-handers hated Cronus with a passion. So Zeus freed the three giants and enlisted their aid in his battle against the early gods. After the Titans had been defeated, Zeus became the leader of a new race of gods, the Olympians. He banished the Titans to Tartarus and appointed Cottus, Briareos, and Gyes to be their jailors. This was a wise strategy. Because the Titans were terrified of the 100-handers, Zeus never again had to worry that his enemies might escape from their dark and gloomy prison.

Gaea's Colossal Warriors

It was perhaps not surprising that Gaea was none too happy that Zeus had defeated and imprisoned her children, the Titans. So she decided to launch a rebellion of her own, this one against the Olympians. To succeed in such a difficult venture, she required fighters who could stand up to the gods, so she turned to the Gigantes. The word "gigantic" derives from their name. They looked very different from the 100-handers. Like the Titans and Olympians, the Gigantes were human-shaped, each with a single head and two arms.

Bloody Beginnings

The origin of the race of Gigantes, as portrayed by ancient writers, was an unusually gruesome event. While he was still in power, the Titan Cronus tried to overthrow his father, Uranus. The head Titan seriously wounded Uranus, causing thousands of blood droplets to fall to Earth. These droplets soon grew into the Gigantes.

Gaea gathered all of these giants and made sure they were loyal to her. Then she unleashed them on Zeus and his Olympians, including Apollo, Athena, Poseidon, Hephaestus, and Dionysus. Zeus' forces also included his semidivine son, the great strongman Heracles. The ancient Greeks called the ensuing battle between gods and giants the Gigantomachy.

The Gigantomachy was Gaea's attempt to gain revenge for Zeus' betrayal and imprisonment of the Titans.

War Begins

As the great battle began, the leader of the giants, Eurymedon, struck the first blow. He hurled a rock as big as a mountaintop at the gods. Then his fellow giants started throwing huge boulders, along with flaming torches made from large trees. Dodging several of these missiles, Zeus tossed a large thunderbolt at a giant named Porphyrion, instantly frying him to death.

Meanwhile, Heracles jumped on the giant Alcyoneus. The two fought desperately until Heracles managed to break his opponent's neck. No sooner had he won that fight than one of the strongest of the giants, Ephialtes, ran at him. Seeing this, Apollo raised his great bow and fired an arrow into the giant's left eye. Ephialtes bellowed in pain, allowing Heracles time to fire an arrow from his own bow. The shaft punctured the giant's other eye, and he collapsed into a heap.

Athena Takes Aim

Seeing his brother giants falling one by one around him, the hot-breathed Enceladus lost his nerve. He attempted to escape the battle. But Athena, the powerful goddess of war, lifted up the entire island of Sicily and hurled it onto him. Some ancient Greek writers claimed that Enceladus survived, trapped forever beneath the island. From time to time thereafter, they said, his burning breath rose from the Sicilian volcano, Mount Etna.

After days of constant, bloody fighting, the Olympians defeated Gaea's colossal warriors. The surviving Gigantes ran for their lives. Then the gods held a feast to commemorate their victory over what they viewed as barbaric beings and forces.

The ancient Greeks believed that Mount Etna's eruptions were created by a giant trapped inside.

Antaeus Meets His Match

Among the multitude of giants that lived during the mythical Age of Heroes, one of the meanest and most deadly was Antaeus. According to legend, he was a son of Poseidon, god of the seas. Antaeus lived far from mainland Greece in the North African region of Libya. When still young he discovered that as long as he had some sort of physical contact with the ground, his strength was tremendous. Regrettably, he used his great power for ill rather than good. Antaeus forced all who visited the area to fight him and he easily killed them all. In another coldhearted act, he used the victims' skulls to roof a temple he was building in honor of his divine father.

Eventually, however, the ruthless Antaeus met his match. One day he noticed a new traveler approaching and hurried out to fight him. The giant did not realize that this stranger was none other than Zeus' son, the famous strongman Heracles. This time, despite his great size and strength, Antaeus found himself in a struggle for his life. The mammoth, brutal brawl shook the earth for miles around. Then Heracles suddenly lifted the giant into the air. This severed Antaeus' vital contact with the ground and eliminated most of his power. Within seconds Heracles caught the giant in a bear hug and crushed the life out of him.

The Biggest Giant

The 100-handers and Gigantes were certainly large creatures. The giants who fought the Olympians towered over the semidivine Heracles, for instance—although his unnaturally great strength allowed him to prevail over them. Yet these early giants were tiny compared to Orion. He was so huge that when he stood in the deepest part of the sea, his head still remained above the surface. That made him well over 1,000 feet (305 meters) tall.

Two myths tried to explain where the formidable Orion came from. One said that his father was Poseidon, god of the seas, and his mother Euryale, daughter of the famous Cretan king Minos. The other story claimed that a ruler of Hyria, in south-central Greece, was unable to have children. So he asked the gods for help. They instructed him to bury a bull's hide deep in the ground and wait. Sure enough, nine months later the infant Orion, already bigger than any adult man, appeared from that spot.

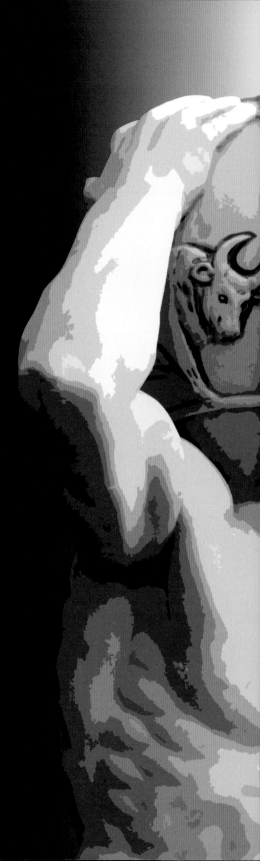

Whoever the young Orion's parents were, he continued to grow at a phenomenal rate. He learned to trap and kill animals and became one of Greece's finest hunters. But like many other mythical giants, he sometimes caused trouble. One ancient account says that he raped the daughter of the king of Chios, a Greek island lying near the coast of Asia Minor. Seeking revenge, the father ordered his soldiers to capture Orion and put out his eyes. But the huge hunter managed to recover his vision by staring directly into the sun.

Another myth about Orion involved the Pleiades. They were the seven daughters of the Titan Atlas, who was renowned for holding Earth upon his back. Perhaps because he wanted to marry one or more of the maidens, Orion relentlessly pursued them. For reasons of his own, Zeus did not want the giant to catch the Pleiades. So the leader of the gods turned both Orion and the seven girls into eternal and separate star groups in the night sky. An alternative myth claims that Artemis, goddess of wild animals and hunting, grew angry with Orion and placed him in the sky. To this day the constellation of Orion remains the brightest and most beautiful of the winter constellations.

The legendary Atlas is often shown carrying either Earth or the heavenly spheres on his shoulders.

The Cyclopes: Giants with a Single Eye

Probably the most familiar of the Greek mythical giants were the Cyclopes. They looked similar to the Olympians and humans except for one important difference. Each Cyclops had a single eye in the middle of his or her forehead.

Two significantly different ancient story lines developed about the Cyclopes. One came from the Greek poet Hesiod. He said that among the many offspring of Gaea and Uranus were three one-eyed giants. Their names were Arges (meaning "Shine,"), Brontes ("Thunderer"), and Steropes ("Lightning-maker"). Uranus was almost as afraid of them as he was of their brothers, the 100-handers. So he locked up the Cyclopes in Tartarus.

Many years later, Hesiod claimed, after Zeus had defeated the Titans, he liberated Arges, Brontes, and Steropes from their captivity. He put them in charge of making the thunderbolts he frequently used as weapons. They also made tridents for the sea god Poseidon.

The Cave of Death

The other ancient story about the Cyclopes came from Hesiod's older contemporary, the poet Homer. In his famous epic, the *Odyssey*, he portrayed the Cyclopes as a race of barbarous giants. They were ill-mannered, at times bloodthirsty, and dwelled in caves on a faraway, rarely visited island.

The story of the *Odyssey* follows the adventures of the hero Odysseus. He was one of the Greek kings who besieged Troy, in northwestern Asia Minor, during the 10-year-long Trojan War. When that conflict ended, he and his men sailed for home. But they were blown off course and eventually landed on the Cyclopes' island. "We came to the land of the Cyclopes," Odysseus later recalled. He added that they were

> a fierce, uncivilized people, who never lift a hand to plant or plow, but put their trust in Providence [God or fate]. [These giants have no] laws, nor any settled customs, but live in hollow caverns in the mountain heights, where each man is lawgiver to his children and his wives, and nobody cares a jot for his neighbors.

Hesiod claimed that the terrible Cyclopes were brothers of the 100-handers. They too were thrown into the Underworld by their horrified father Uranus.

The brutal giant Cyclops Polyphemus killed and ate six of Odysseus' men.

Name:
Polyphemus

Roman name:
Polyphemus

Appearance:
a giant with a single eye

Family:
son of the sea god Poseidon; one of several Cyclopes

Famous myth:
capturing Odysseus and 12 Greeks in his cave

Also famous for:
being blinded by Odysseus and his men

The Greeks badly needed food, so Odysseus selected 12 men and went ashore. Soon they came upon a large cave with many goats and sheep inside. The men hoped to gather up several of the animals and hurry back to their ship before anyone noticed.

But just as they prepared to leave with the livestock, the Cyclops who lived in the cave came home. His name was Polyphemus. Seeing the intruders, the ugly, smelly giant quickly pushed an immense rock across the cave entrance, trapping the Greeks inside. Fearfully, the men tried to keep out of the Cyclops' clutches, but he was able to grab hold of two of them. He smashed their heads against the floor, causing their skulls to crack open and their brains to fall out. Then he tore their bodies apart with his bare hands and ate them, bones and all, while the other Greeks watched in horror.

Odysseus thought hard about what to do next. They could wait until the giant fell asleep, he reasoned, then stab him to death with their swords. But that would only seal their doom. They lacked the strength to move the huge rock. So the giant had to remain alive until he had moved the rock and cleared the entrance to this cave of death.

First blinding him with a wooden beam, Odysseus and his men tricked the Cyclops.

"Nobody"

The next day Polyphemus devoured two more of Odysseus' men for breakfast and two more for supper. Then the giant made a fire to stay warm and started gulping down enormous amounts of wine. At one point he turned to Odysseus and asked him what his name was. But Odysseus, who was known for his cleverness, was already hatching a plan and lied. He claimed that his name was Nobody.

Eventually the wine went to Polyphemus' head and caused him to doze off. Odysseus then set the rest of his scheme in motion. He and his remaining six men used their swords to carve one end of a large wooden beam until it was sharp. Next they heated the pointed tip in the fire. Finally, together they lifted the beam and with all their strength jammed it into the giant's single eye. "The blood boiled up around the burning wood," Odysseus later remembered. "The fiery smoke from the blazing eyeball singed his lids and brow all round, and the very roots of his eye crackled in the heat."

Cyclops Wakes

Polyphemus awakened with a jolt and screamed in agony. Yanking the beam from his mangled eye socket, he thrashed aimlessly around the cave. Then he began yelling for the Cyclopes who dwelled nearby to come to his aid. A few minutes later, several other giants arrived on the far side of the great rock. They called out to Polyphemus and asked who had injured him. Thinking quickly, the wounded Cyclops recalled the name Odysseus had given him earlier. Over and over again, he angrily shouted that Nobody had injured him. Hearing this, Polyphemus' neighbors figured that he'd had too much to drink and went home.

Just as Odysseus had hoped, the next morning the Cyclops removed the great rock from the cave entrance. As he did every day, the giant allowed his sheep and goats to go outside and graze in the fields. Odysseus cleverly arranged that he and his men should cling to the undersides of the animals as they left so that the blind Polyphemus could not detect them. Using every ounce of strength they could muster, the men sprinted to their ship and climbed aboard. They counted themselves lucky to have survived their encounter with one of the most dangerous of the strange creatures of the bygone age that Homer described.

Chapter 4
HIDEOUS, BLOODTHIRSTY MONSTERS

A great many monsters existed during the legendary Age of Heroes. Most were hideous, many were bloodthirsty, and all posed a threat to either humans or the gods. Perhaps the earliest of these dangerous creatures to appear was Typhon (or Typhoeus). It had 100 heads, each like that of a huge snake. Typhon also had many sounds to go with its many heads. Sometimes it barked like a dog, while other times it roared like an enraged bull.

Son of Tartarus

Typhon's mother was Gaea, the great spirit that inhabited Earth. The beast's father was said to have been Tartarus, the deepest, darkest region of the Underworld. At the dawn of time, that gloomy place had a life force of its own.

The Flying Furies

Some of the more frightening monsters in the Greek myths were the Furies. That most common name for them derives from their later Roman name—Furiae. To the Greeks, they were the Erinyes. Flying creatures with sharp teeth and claws, they often carried lit torches and whips with which they tortured their victims. Those victims were almost always criminals. In particular, the Furies hunted down murderers, especially those who had killed a parent, sibling, or other family member. The creatures appear prominently in The Eumenides, a classic play by the ancient Athenian writer Aeschylus. In the story they relentlessly pursue a young man named Orestes. He had killed his mother, Clytemnestra, to get revenge for her murder of his father. In the play's finale, the goddess Athena steps in and changes the Furies into benevolent creatures— the Eumenides, the "kindly ones."

A Frightening Battle

For the most part, monsters such as Typhon were born to kill. Realizing this, Gaea took advantage of her offspring's large size, strength, and destructive abilities. She had long harbored a grudge against Zeus, leader of the Olympian gods, and had tried, but failed, to kill him. When Typhon was fully grown, she tried again. Gaea instructed the creature to attack Zeus and tear him limb from limb.

The mighty Zeus saw Typhon coming, however. Grasping one his trademark thunderbolts, the god hurled it at the 100-headed monster. Stunned for a moment, Typhon stopped. But soon it regained its bearings and charged at Zeus again. Undaunted and unafraid of the beast, the god launched several more thunderbolts. One ancient account claimed that while the frightening battle raged most of the other gods fled southward to Egypt. They disguised themselves as animals. This supposedly explained why so many of the Egyptian gods looked like animals.

Injured Typhon

Eventually, according to the ancient Greek poet Hesiod, Zeus managed to severely injure Typhon. The god's blazing thunderbolts set the monster afire, causing it to scream in agony. "The whole Earth boiled," Hesiod recalled.

> Great waves raged along the shore at [Zeus'] charge. [The god] raised up his strength [and] burned the dreadful monster's ghastly heads. [He] threw him down, all maimed, and the earth groaned . . . And angry in his heart, Zeus hurled him down to Tartarus.

Though defeated, Typhon was far from dead. In centuries following the great battle, from time to time Typhon let out many huge breaths. Legends say that these rose from the depths of Tartarus and became typhoons, great storms named after Typhon. "As evil storms they rage," Hesiod wrote. "Each blows in season, scattering ships and killing sailors."

Typhon, a 100-headed beast, was no match for Zeus. But he survived Zeus' attacks and later created huge storms known as typhoons.

Huge Hound of Hell

Typhon also left behind an appalling offspring called Cerberus. In many of the Greek myths Cerberus was a huge, extremely vicious dog— a repulsive monster born of equally repulsive monsters. While Typhon was its father, another horrifying beast, Echidna, was its mother. Most ancient accounts claimed the huge hound had three heads. Hesiod was alone in saying that Cerberus had 50 heads.

Cerberus was said to guard the entrance to the Underworld. The creature carefully watched as the shades of dead people trudged through that portal of no return. If a person attempted to run away and escape his fate, Cerberus seized and ate him.

The most famous myth about Cerberus involved Heracles, who was half human and half god. A king named Eurystheus assigned the hero 12 fantastically difficult tasks. They included slaying the Hydra, a nine-headed monster, taming a herd of man-eating horses, and cleaning a group of unbelievably filthy cattle stables.

Descent into the Underworld

Eventually Eurystheus ordered Heracles to descend into the Underworld, capture Cerberus, and bring the monstrous dog back to Greece. The strongman did not know how to find the shadowy underground kingdom. So two gods—Athena and Hermes—guided him to it. The Styx river marked the boundary between the Underworld and the human world. There was only one way to cross the river's murky waters. That was to summon Charon. A stern boatman wearing a dark robe and hood, he ferried souls from the land of the living to the land of the dead.

Seeing Heracles waiting on the shore, Charon realized who the man was and that he was alive. The boatman was only supposed to ferry the dead across the river. But he had heard about the hero's enormous strength and did not want to test it. Without raising a fuss, therefore, Charon silently transported Heracles to the river's far side.

Charon transported souls across the Styx river before their descent into the Underworld.

Name:
Hades

Roman name:
Pluto

Group of gods:
Olympian

Family:
son of Cronus and Gaea;
brother of Zeus; uncle
of Heracles

Responsibility:
the Underworld

Symbols:
his dog Cerberus, cap
of invisibility

Uncle against Nephew

Stepping off Charon's boat, the strongman soon encountered
a much more formidable character than the grim ferryman.
As Heracles watched, a large dark shape loomed up and blocked
his path. In the dim light, the man recognized that shape as
his relative, Hades, lord of the Underworld. (Because Heracles
was the son of Zeus, and Zeus and Hades were brothers,
Hades was Heracles' uncle.)

Hades demanded to know why his nephew had intruded into
the realm of the dead. The man explained that he had come to
get the monstrous dog Cerberus. This was completely out of the
question, Hades said. Heracles must immediately turn around
and go back to the land of the living. But the burly son of Zeus
was not used to taking no for an answer. Without warning he
leaped forward and wrestled his uncle to the ground, injuring
him in the process.

Hades now changed his tune and agreed to allow Heracles to
capture the enormous guard dog. There was one condition,
however. The man had to accomplish the task without any
weapons, using muscle power alone. Hades evidently thought
that it would be impossible to capture Cerberus without the use
of weapons. But he was wrong. Heracles was able to seize the
monster, lock it in a cage, and cart it up to Earth's surface.

Finally the strongman presented Cerberus to King Eurystheus.
The ruler was astounded that Heracles had been able to
accomplish a task that everyone had assumed was impossible.
Quite naturally, Eurystheus did not want to keep such a
dangerous gift. So he ordered that Cerberus be returned
to the Underworld, and Heracles once more obeyed.

Heracles managed to capture the monstrous three-headed dog, Cerberus, that guarded the Underworld.

Slaying the Hydra

The Hydra was a mythical monster having a large, slimy, snakelike body and nine heads. If someone cut off one of the heads, one or two rapidly grew back, which made the creature difficult to kill. The Hydra terrorized people in the region around Lerna, in southeastern Greece. It killed and devoured cattle and destroyed farms until finally the heroic strongman Heracles slew it. That act fulfilled the second of the 12 labors to which he had been sentenced. The ancient Greek writer Apollodorus of Athens described the incident:

The monstrous serpentlike Hydra had nine heads, each with vile, poisonous breath.

Heracles went to Lerna [and] found the Hydra on the brow of a hill [where the beast] had its den. Shooting at it with flaming arrows, Heracles drove the creature out, and then, when it came close, he grabbed it and held it tight. But the Hydra wrapped itself around his foot, and he was not able to get free by striking off its heads with his club, for as soon as one head was cut off, two grew in its place. [Eventually] by burning the stumps of the Hydra's heads with firebrands, [the strongman] kept them from growing out again.

Crete's Minotaur

Cerberus was a monstrous form of an ordinary animal, a dog. Similarly, another famous mythical monster was a hideous version of a familiar creature, a bull. It was most commonly called the Minotaur. Its name was short for Minotauros, meaning "bull of Minos." Its keeper was King Minos, ruler of Crete. The beast had the head of a bull and the body of a man, so it walked on two feet. It also regularly feasted on human flesh.

The manner in which the Minotaur came to be was both strange and unnatural. One day Minos prayed to Poseidon, lord of the seas, and asked for a special bull that the king could sacrifice to the gods. Poseidon sent the bull, which was an unusually handsome creature. It was so striking, in fact, that Minos spared it from death. Moreover, his wife, Pasiphae, developed an abnormal passion for the bull. She then mated with it, producing the Minotaur.

Pasiphae would not allow her strange offspring to be killed. So Minos ordered his talented servant, Daedalus, to construct an underground maze to house the Minotaur. That maze came to be called the Labyrinth.

Theseus in the Labyrinth

The best-known myth about the Minotaur described what it ate and how it met its end. The story began when King Minos' son, Androgeus, died in Athens, the leading city on the Greek mainland. Minos unfairly blamed the Athenian king, Aegeus, for the youth's death. To get revenge, the Cretan ruler, who was more powerful than Aegeus, forced the Athenian king to agree to a cruel arrangement. Every year Athens had to send seven boys and seven girls to Crete. Minos locked these youths inside the Labyrinth, where the hungry Minotaur ate them one by one.

Fortunately for the Athenians, Aegeus had a strong and courageous son named Theseus. The young man offered to accompany the next batch of hostages to Crete, where he would do his best to save them. In the words of the ancient Greek writer Plutarch:

> Theseus urged his father to take heart and boasted that he would overcome the Minotaur, and so Aegeus gave the [ship's] pilot a [white] sail [and] ordered him on the return voyage to hoist the white canvas if Theseus were safe, but otherwise to [raise a] black [sail] as a sign of mourning.

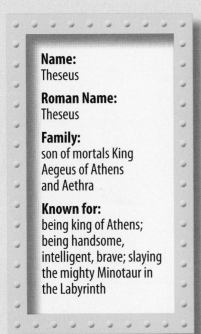

Name:
Theseus

Roman Name:
Theseus

Family:
son of mortals King Aegeus of Athens and Aethra

Known for:
being king of Athens; being handsome, intelligent, brave; slaying the mighty Minotaur in the Labyrinth

The Minotaur of Crete was a powerful and terrifying creature.

Theseus fulfilled his mission. When he arrived in Crete, he allowed King Minos' soldiers to lead him to the Labyrinth. Along the way, he met Minos' daughter, Ariadne. As luck would have it, she fell in love with Theseus at first sight.

Wanting to save Theseus from certain death, Ariadne secretly asked Daedalus how a person might escape from the maze in which the Minotaur dwelled. Daedalus gave her a ball of thread and told her to attach one end to the door of the Labyrinth. Whoever entered the maze should unravel the thread as he walked. That way he could follow the thread to make it back to the entrance. Ariadne then gave Theseus the ball of thread and a sword. Noted scholar Michael Grant tells what happened next:

> Leaving his companions near the entrance, Theseus advanced to the center of the Labyrinth, playing out his thread. When he came upon the Minotaur, he killed it, using the sword or, according to another version [of the myth,] his fists. [Following the unraveled thread], he then returned to the entrance, where Ariadne released the [hostages] from the Labyrinth, and they made their way back to the Athenian ship [and] set sail for home.

Unfortunately, Theseus and his companions were so busy celebrating their success that they forgot to replace the black sail with a white one. As the vessel neared Athens' port, King Aegeus saw the black sail and assumed his son was dead. In a fit of grief, the ruler threw himself into the sea, which thereafter bore the name Aegean in his honor.

The daughter of King Minos, Ariadne, helped Theseus to escape from the Labyrinth.

The Harpies were hideous to behold and repulsive in every way.

Foul-smelling Harpies

All mythical monsters smelled bad. But none had a fouler stench than the Harpies. They were hideous and disgusting birdlike beasts with wings, women's faces, and sharp claws. The Greeks sometimes called them Snatchers because they frequently flew down and stole people's food before they could eat it. The Harpies were also known to drip their bodily fluids onto human food, making it too repulsive to eat.

The Harpies appear in a myth about the hero Jason and his crewmen, the Argonauts. While searching for the famous Golden Fleece, they came upon a starving old man named Phineus. He told them that the Harpies snatched his food at almost every meal.

Jason and his men decided to help the unfortunate fellow. When the creatures next swooped down to grab Phineus' food, two of the Argonauts, Zetes and Calais, attacked them. The Harpies fled and the men pursued them. They were about to slay the smelly beasts when Iris, goddess of the rainbow, appeared. Saying that she was the Harpies' sister, she made a bargain with Zetes and Calais. If they would spare the monstrous creatures, she would keep them away from Phineus. The deal was struck, and the Harpies never bothered the old man again.

The Monstrous Riddle-Teller

Most mythical monsters could not speak. One monster that was able to talk was the Sphinx. More than 10 feet (3 meters) tall, the Sphinx had wings, the body of a lion, and the head of a woman. It told each of its cornered victims a riddle. If the person knew the correct answer, he could go free. But if he could not solve the riddle, the creature immediately devoured him.

The merciless monster terrorized people in one village or town after another until it reached the Greek city of Thebes. Each time it grabbed hold of a Theban farmer or merchant, it posed the riddle. But none of them could solve it, so they ended up in the creature's stomach.

Finally a courageous young man named Oedipus arrived in Thebes. The Sphinx approached him and presented the riddle: "What creature is first four-footed, then two-footed, and finally three-footed?" The clever Oedipus quickly responded with the right answer. "That creature is a man," he stated. "In infancy, he crawls on all fours, making him four-footed; when grown, he walks on two feet; and as an old man he uses a cane, in a sense a third foot."

The Sphinx was astounded that the man had solved the riddle. Humiliated at having been outwitted by a mere human, the monster screamed at the top of its lungs. Some ancient accounts claim it found a sword and stabbed itself through the heart. Others say it jumped off a cliff to its death. Either way, the Thebans were relieved to be rid of the beast.

The Sphinx was a winged hybrid creature. It loved riddles but was finally outwitted by a mortal.

Name:
Medusa

Roman name:
Medusa

Appearance:
Gorgon, gross monstrous female, with snakes for hair

Family:
daughter of sea creatures Phorcys and Ceto; sister of Stheno and Euryale

Famous myth:
anyone who looked at her would turn into stone

Also famous for:
being beheaded by hero Perseus

Once a beautiful woman, Medusa was turned into a foul creature with snakes for hair and a deadly stare.

A Monster Too Ugly to Look At

Being female and having a woman's face, the Sphinx had something in common with another mythical monster—Medusa. According to Greek legend, Medusa was one of three sisters called the Gorgons. They were the daughters of two sea creatures, Phorcys and Ceto, who themselves had been conceived by Gaea, the primitive spirit inhabiting Earth. The other two Gorgons were Stheno and Euryale.

A number of ancient accounts said that Medusa was originally a beautiful young woman. That beauty attracted the attention of Poseidon, god of the seas. One day the two made love in one of the temples dedicated to the goddess of wisdom, Athena. She caught them in the act and was enraged. To punish Medusa, the goddess turned her into a gross, misshapen being with a mass of squirming snakes in place of her hair. Moreover, if a person looked directly at the Gorgon's face, he or she turned to stone in mere seconds. In a sense, therefore, Medusa became a monster too ugly to look at.

Eventually Medusa came to live, along with her sisters—who were unaffected by gazing at her—on a remote island. Over the years travelers landed on the island by accident or to search for food. All of them made the mistake of looking at the snake-haired creature that dwelled there. So they became statuelike pillars frozen forever in various poses.

The Invisible Intruder

The day finally came, however, when a man landed on the Gorgons' island and managed to survive. Named Perseus, he had been sent by Polydectus, king of the Aegean island of Seriphos, to kill Medusa. The young man had several advantages during his quest. First, Hermes, the messenger god, guided him to the island. According to the ancient Roman poet and storyteller Ovid, Perseus traveled through

> thick-bearded forests, and tearing rocks and stones, until he found the Gorgons' home. And as he looked about from left to right, no matter where he turned, he saw both man and beast turned into stone, all creatures who had seen Medusa's face.

Perseus' second advantage was a highly polished metal shield given to him by Athena, goddess of war. Other gifts he'd recently received included a pair of winged sandals that enabled him to fly and a cap that made anyone who wore it invisible. With these objects, Perseus set out to confront Medusa.

Soon the young man found his prey sleeping on a big rock. Careful not to look directly at Medusa's face, he gazed at her reflection in the mirrorlike shield. Suddenly the hideous monster woke up. She could sense that an intruder was near, but could not see Perseus thanks to his cap of invisibility. His winged sandals allowed him to circle the Gorgon from above. Tightly gripping his sharpened sword, he dived at her at just the right moment. A swift slash of the sword severed the snake-haired head from Medusa's body. While her body spurted blood and collapsed in a heap, Perseus swooped sideways and caught her head in a sack.

Birth of Pegasus

Having successfully completed his mission, Perseus flew away, making sure not to peek at the sack's deadly contents. At the last moment, though, he looked back at the blood-soaked body on the rock. To the young man's astonishment, something was fighting its way out of the corpse. While Perseus watched in awe, a magnificent winged horse rose. It glanced around to get its first glimpse of the world. Then the stunning creature, which would come to be known as Pegasus, briefly tested its wings and gracefully fluttered away. As Perseus departed in the other direction, he was struck by an important realization. Even a being as monstrous and lethal as Medusa could harbor deep inside it an element of wondrous beauty.

MONSTERS AND CREATURES

The monsters and creatures of Greek myths were often fusions of two or more creatures.

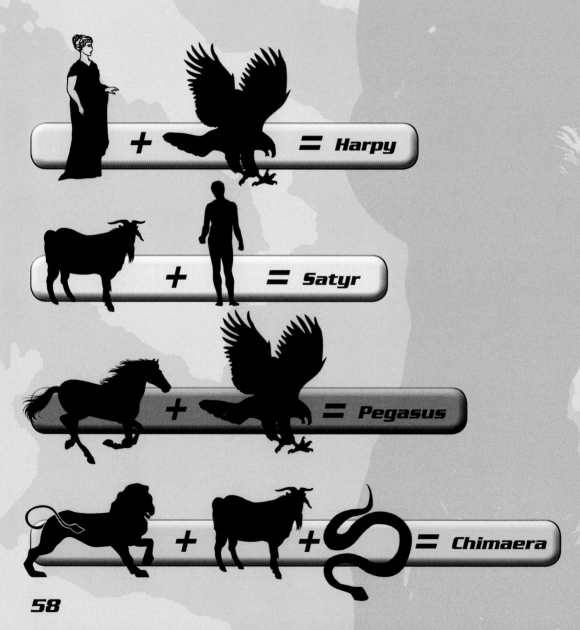

+ = **Harpy**

+ = **Satyr**

+ = **Pegasus**

+ + = **Chimaera**

+ = Centaur

+ = Griffin

+ = Minotaur

+ + = Sphinx

+ = Gorgon

ADDITIONAL RESOURCES

Further Reading

Daly, Kathleen N. *Greek and Roman Mythology A to Z.*
New York: Chelsea House, 2009.

Hamby, Zachary. *Mythology for Teens: Classic Myths for Today's World.*
Austin, Texas: Prufrock Press, 2009.

Hile, Kevin. *Centaur.*
Farmington Hills, Mich.: Kidhaven Press, 2008.

Kurth, Steve. *Hercules: The Twelve Labors.*
Minneapolis: Graphic Universe, 2007.

Pearce, Q.L. *Pegasus.*
Farmington Hills, Mich.: Kidhaven Press, 2008.

Storrie, Paul D. *Perseus: The Hunt for Medusa's Head: A Greek Myth.*
Minneapolis: Graphic Universe, 2009.

Internet Sites

Use FactHound to find Internet sites related to this book. All of the sites on FactHound have been researched by our staff.

Here's all you do:
Visit *www.facthound.com*
Type in this code:
9780756544812

GLOSSARY

Age of Heroes the period of the distant past in which the classical Greeks believed the stories told in their myths took place. Modern scholars call that era Greece's late Bronze Age and date it from about 1500 BC to 1150 BC.

Argonauts the crew of the *Argo,* the ancient Greek hero Jason's ship

banish to send or drive away

barbarism brutal or coarse acts

centaur a mythical creature that was half man and half horse

civilized cultured or educated

classical Greeks modern scholars date Greece's Classical Age to about 500 BC to 323 BC. More generally, the inhabitants of Greece between about 800 BC and 300 BC.

constellation groups of stars seen from Earth. Many were named by the ancient Greeks for animals or mythological beings.

Cyclops (plural Cyclopes) a mythical giant having a single eye in the middle of its forehead

epic a long poem, usually describing heroic acts

equine resembling a horse

fertility being fertile, or able to produce offspring

fleece the woolen coat of a sheep or goat

griffin a mythical creature with four legs, wings, and a beak like that of a bird

Harpies mythical flying creatures with sharp claws and beaks

hybrid the result of mixing two animal species

labyrinth a maze; In Greek mythology the Labyrinth was a mass of rooms on Crete that housed the fearsome Minotaur

medieval related to the Middle Ages, generally from AD mid-400s to the mid-1400s

Minotaur a mythical creature that was half man and half bull

mythology a group of stories about gods, monsters, heroes, and strangely shaped or fantastic creatures

nymph a minor nature goddess

Olympians the group of gods led by Zeus and thought to live on top of Mount Olympus, Greece's highest mountain

prophecy the art or process of foretelling the future; or a specific prediction

ruthless hardhearted, showing no kindness

satyr a mythical creature that was half man and half goat

shade the soul or spirit of a dead person

Sphinx a mythical monster having the body of a lion, wings, and a woman's face

symbol something that stands for or represents something else

Titans a race of gods that ruled the universe before the rise of the Olympians

trident a three-pronged spear; it was one of the symbols of the sea god Poseidon

typhoon a hurricane

uncivilized barbaric, or uncultured and uneducated

SOURCE NOTES

Chapter 1
Where Reality and Fantasy Dissolve

Page 6, line 5: Edith Hamilton. *Mythology*. New York: Grand Central, 1999, p. 19.

Page 7, line 21: Stewart Perowne. "Introduction" to Michael Stapleton, *The Illustrated Dictionary of Greek and Roman Mythology*. New York: Peter Bedrick, 1988, p. 7.

Chapter 2
Half-humans and Other Odd Creatures

Page 14, line 14: Diodorus Siculus. *Library of History*. Quoted in Theoi Greek Mythology, Satyroi. 14 April 2011.
www.theoi.com/Georgikos/Satyroi.html

Chapter 3
Multitudes of Monstrous Giants

Page 20, line 13: Michael Stapleton. *The Illustrated Dictionary of Greek and Roman Mythology*. New York: P. Bedrick Books, 1986, p. 84.

Page 30, col. 2, line 15: Homer. *Odyssey*. Trans. E.V. Rieu. Baltimore: Penguin, 1967, p. 142.

Page 35, line 6: Ibid, p. 150.

Chapter 4
Hideous, Bloodthirsty Monsters

Page 39, line 5: Hesiod. *Theogony*, in *Hesiod and Theognis*. Trans. Dorothea Wender. New York: Penguin, 1973, p. 51.

Page 39, line 18: Ibid, p. 51.

Page 45, line 1: Apollodorus. *Library*. Quoted in *Classical Gods and Heroes: Myths as Told by the Ancient Authors*. New York: Morrow Quill, 1974, p. 157.

Page 47, line 20: Plutarch. *Life of Theseus,* in *The Rise and Fall of Athens: Nine Greek Lives by Plutarch*. Trans. Ian Scott-Kilvert. New York: Penguin, 1984, p. 24.

Page 49, line 14: Michael Grant and John Hazel. *Who's Who in Classical Mythology*. London: Routledge, 2002, pp. 395–396.

Page 56, line 8: Ovid. *Metamorphoses*. Trans. Rolfe Humphries. Bloomington: Indiana University Press, 1967, p. 134.

SELECT BIBLIOGRAPHY

Ancient Sources

Hendricks, Rhoda A., ed. and trans. *Classical Gods and Heroes: Myths as Told by the Ancient Authors*. New York: Morrow Quill, 1974.

Hesiod. *Theogony*, in *Hesiod and Theognis*. Trans. Dorothea Wender. New York: Penguin, 1973.

Homer. *Odyssey*. Trans. E.V. Rieu. Baltimore: Penguin, 1967.

Knox, Bernard M.W., ed. *The Norton Book of Classical Literature*. New York: W.W. Norton, 1993.

Ovid. *Metamorphoses*. Trans. Rolfe Humphries. Bloomington: Indiana University Press, 1967.

Plutarch. *Life of Theseus, in The Rise and Fall of Athens: Nine Greek Lives by Plutarch*. Trans. Ian Scott-Kilvert. New York: Penguin, 1984.

Sophocles. *Oedipus the King*. Trans. Bernard M.W. Knox. New York: Simon and Schuster, 2005.

Modern Sources

Bellingham, David. *An Introduction to Greek Mythology*. Secaucus, N.J.: Chartwell Books, 2002.

Fitton, J. Lesley. *The Discovery of the Greek Bronze Age*. Cambridge, Mass.: Harvard University Press, 2001.

Grant, Michael. *A Guide to the Ancient World*. New York: Barnes and Noble, 1986.

Grant, Michael. *Myths of the Greeks and Romans*. New York: Plume, 1995.

Grant, Michael, and John Hazel. *Who's Who in Classical Mythology*. London: Routledge, 2002.

Hamilton, Edith. *Mythology*. New York: Grand Central, 1999.

Morford, Mark P.O., and Robert J. Lenardon. *Classical Mythology*. New York: Oxford University Press, 2010.

Nardo, Don. *Greenhaven Encyclopedia of Greek and Roman Mythology*. San Diego: Greenhaven Press, 2002.

Padgett, J. Michael. *The Centaur's Smile: The Human Animal in Early Greek Art*. Princeton, N.J.: Princeton University Art Museum, 2003.

Stapleton, Michael. *The Illustrated Dictionary of Greek and Roman Mythology*. New York: Peter Bedrick, 1988.

INDEX

About the author

Noted historian Don Nardo specializes in the ancient world and has published numerous books about Greek, Roman, Mesopotamian, and Egyptian mythology. He lives with his wife, Christine, in Massachusetts.